Allosaurus!

The Life and Death of Big Al

Adapted by Stephen Cole

DUTTON

Who Was Big Al?

Imagine that the world has become a giant safari park with no people in it. Imagine that instead of lions and elephants, it is teeming with monsters.

Between 250 and 65 million years ago, that's exactly the kind of place the world was. During the **Mesozoic** era, strange **reptiles** battled for survival on the land, in the sea, and in the sky. It was the time of the **dinosaurs**.

We know these creatures existed because of **fossils**. And in 1991 the fossilized skeleton of a practically complete *Allosaurus* was uncovered by a fossil-collecting company in Wyoming. Since the discovery was made on public land that they had accidentally strayed onto, the fossil belonged to the nation. Arrangements were made to excavate the *Allosaurus*, soon nicknamed Big Al by experts.

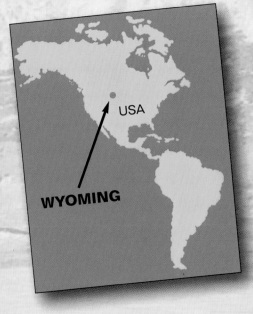

USA

WYOMING

It took eight days to fully reveal Big Al, using tools such as hammers, chisels, and brushes. The bones were numbered and their position in the rock noted. Then they were treated with chemical preservatives and wrapped in plaster "bandages" so that they could be transported safely for further study.

Al lived around 145 million years ago, right at the end of the **Jurassic** period. *Allosaurus* had certain similarities to *Tyrannosaurus rex:* a taste for flesh, needle-sharp teeth, and two legs that let it chase its prey at high speeds.

Now, using the latest in medical scanners, forensic examination, knowledge of animal behavior, and evidence from other fossil sites, scientists have been able to piece together the story of Big Al's life and death.

This book not only tells Al's amazing story, but also answers important questions about the scientific evidence behind it. As you read, you'll find that certain words are printed in bold type. Look them up in the Fact File on pages 44 to 47.

You probably already know what dinosaurs are. But you've never actually known a dinosaur.

Until now...

The Hatchling

Inside an egg, buried in the warm Jurassic sand, a reptile eye flickers open. It is pitch-black in here, stifling. Now almost a foot long, the tiny creature has grown too big, the egg cannot contain him. It's time to hatch.

His head strains against the shell, and pushes through it, into dirt and darkness. He struggles to be free, but the sand is too heavy to shift. The **hatchling** opens his mouth for the first time and screams out to the waiting world above for help. His mother will never name him, but we will know this baby *Allosaurus* as Big Al.

How do we know that Allosaurus laid eggs?

Since most reptiles—including crocodiles, who originated during the dinosaur era—lay eggs, and since dinosaurs were reptiles, we would expect them to do the same. Birds lay eggs, too, of course, and new research shows that birds are even more closely related to dinosaurs than crocodiles. The oldest bird, **Archaeopteryx**, had feathers and wings. But its skeleton is very similar to those of small flesh-eating dinosaurs such as **Deinonychus** and **Velociraptor.**

Proof that *Allosaurus* laid eggs came recently when a nest of over 100 fossilized dinosaur eggs from the late Jurassic was discovered in Portugal. Examination of the tiny skeletons inside the eggs shows that they were laid by a dinosaur that looked much like Al.

Survival Bond

Al's mother hears his cries.
As an adult *Allosaurus*, she is
the largest **predator** of the
Jurassic period, fierce, savage,
and feared the world over.
But right now, she is gentle
and tender as she shuffles dirt
away from the nest to reveal
the eggs underneath. She
knows her children need her.

Not-so-big-Al is one of
many hatchlings in the nest.
He glimpses patches of deep
blue sky as the roof of the
nest is cleared away; then his
mother's head dips down to
greet him. She bathes him in
sticky saliva so he will smell like her. Now the mother will recognize Al
as her own, and look out for him while he is small and weak—instead of
eating him alive as she would any other defenseless creature.

Why did Allosaurus mothers put their scent on their hatchlings?

Crocodiles use their strong sense of smell to recognize their hatchlings and protect them until they can defend themselves. Experts think *Allosaurus* mothers would have behaved in the same way, marking their young with a familiar scent.

Fast Food

Al and his fellow hatchlings may now be safe from their mother, but they are still in danger. Any hatchling foolish enough to wander too far from its mother will make a tasty treat for the *Ornitholestes* watching it from the forest nearby.

Al's mother senses the danger and leads her children away from the nest. They journey deeper into the forest. It is time for the hatchlings to learn how to hunt for themselves.

A dragonfly hovers busily over the hatchlings' heads. The mother watches as her children jump through the air, trying to close their jaws on the insect, hunger making the tiny **carnivores** faster, sharper, deadlier.

How do we know what baby dinosaurs ate?

Fossils of young dinosaur carnivores have little peglike teeth, very different from the  pointed teeth used by grown-ups to slice through meat. These tiny teeth were used to grind up insects, a high-energy prehistoric baby food.

Tasty Treat

Not only insects will fill Al's stomach now that he's growing. His little eyes narrow as he spots a new meal scuttling across the forest floor toward him—a lizard. The lizard darts up a tree as Al hops nimbly around it.

Al reaches up and grabs the tiny reptile with his powerful jaws.

But before he can eat it, his brothers and sisters suddenly decide it's time to join in. A fight breaks out as they squabble over bits of the lizard's scaly body. Each of the hatchlings needs plenty of food in order to grow. Until they are big enough to scare off other dinosaurs, they are constantly at risk of becoming lunch themselves.

How quickly did a dinosaur grow?

Crocodiles and birds grow to their full size fast so that they can survive. By looking inside a collection of *Allosaurus* leg bones of different sizes and comparing the structure to the bones of crocodiles and birds, experts know that *Allosaurus* grew quickly, too. Al would have become a 19½-foot teenager by the time he was just five years old.

Death in the Family

The setting sun is bleeding streaks of scarlet over the sky. The river is still as shadows start to fall. The hatchlings are playing together, darting in and out of the trees.

So, when the *Ornitholestes* darts out of the bushes, the hatchlings don't see it coming until it's too late. Al squeals as the huge, savage jaws swing down toward him, and dives for cover. He hides in the undergrowth, trembling as the predator crashes around him and the other hatchlings cry out for help. Then one of the screams dies off. There is the sound of bones crunching, and the *Ornitholestes* charges back into the forest.

Another cry sounds, deeper, louder. It is a voice Al runs to, the voice of his mother, coming to look for her children. The hatchlings gather around, but the mother knows that one will never come back. She strides away, her surviving children bobbing about her legs as if tied there with string.

If hatchlings made such easy meals, why didn't dinosaurs become extinct sooner?

Because they laid lots of eggs—from 8 to 100. Many, but not all, of their offspring would be eaten before they were fully grown. Just as in the wilderness today, the dinosaur world was full of hungry predators.

Hunter and the Hunted

One year later, Al has grown to be almost ten feet long and has left
the protection of his mother. Now he must look out for himself.
His diet of lizards and small animals is no longer enough; he needs
more meat—and that means hunting dinosaurs.

Peering through some bushes, Al spies a group of plant-eating
Othnielia. The adults are too big for him to tackle, but the babies
make a tempting target. He narrows his eyes, tenses his body
for the attack, and fixes his sights on his chosen victim.

Then Al sprints from the cover of the forest. But he is too noisy, too slow—he has no experience in this kind of hunt. At lightning speed, the *Othnielia* scatter at the sound of him. Al snaps at the tail of one, but misses. Before he can turn and chase after the **herbivores**, they have all vanished.

Were carnivorous dinosaurs fussy eaters?

Not at all. They counted anything as meat—even their own kind, which they saw as competition in the search for food.

Were plant-eating dinosaurs an easy target?

No. Herbivores were well-equipped to deal with predators. Othnielia, for example, were very fast. **Stegosaurus** had armored plates and lethal clublike tails, while **Brachiosaurus** and **Apatosaurus** had size and weight on their side.

A Tempting Trap

Al stalks back into the forest, still hungry. But then his nose twitches as a new scent wafts over. He follows it to a muddy pool, and discovers the half-submerged corpse of a massive *Stegosaurus*. There's another *Stegosaurus* in the pool, too, bellowing angrily.

Al would move in for the kill, but he's frightened off by a large *Allosaurus* that is already wading in. Al is too small to clash with this adult.

The *Stegosaurus* is not warning others away—it is shrieking in frustration because it is stuck in quicksand.

How do we know that dinosaurs got stuck in quicksand traps like this one?

At a site in Utah, the fossils of at least 44 *Allosaurus* were found, along with a few *Stegosaurus*. The rock at this site is mudstone, suggesting that the area was once quicksand. It seems likely that the dinosaurs ended up here exactly as Al observed.

A Sticky End

The *Allosaurus* wading into the pool is sinking into the quicksand, powerless to escape. Many more carnivores will be lured into this trap by the sight and smell of dead and dying *Stegosaurus,* and will in turn die here, slowly, painfully—food for the **pterosaurs** swooping down from above.

Al is more scared by the attack of a bigger dinosaur than he is by the quicksand. He turns and leaves, his belly rumbling as he hunts out other, easier prey.

How clever were Allosaurus?

Not very. Examination of a fossilized *Allosaurus* brain through medical scanners shows it to be very similar to a crocodile's brain. A crocodile has a strong sense of smell, but not much brainpower. If something smells tasty, a crocodile will go for it and eat it, whatever it is, without thinking. An *Allosaurus* would probably have behaved in just the same way.

An Allosaurus skull, and a cast of the inside showing brain size and shape

Watching and Waiting

Four years pass, during which time Al grows bigger, meaner, and faster. Now, at five years of age, he is not yet fully grown, but few dinosaurs would want to tangle with him. He is almost twenty feet long!

Al is stalking his next meal.

A herd of **Diplodocus** is trudging across a lake of salt. They are in search of fresh vegetation to feed their enormous stomachs. It is a long journey through tough conditions for the *Diplodocus*, and the weakest animals may not make it.

Al, along with many other hungry *Allosaurus*, is here to see to it that they don't.

The herd is disturbed by the nearby predators. One of the *Diplodocus* is sick, and the *Allosaurus* work together as a pack to bring it down. Al leads the charge, and the chase is on…

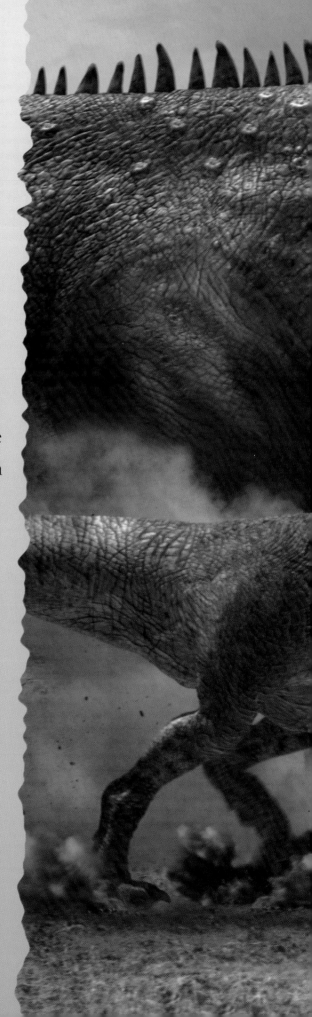

How do we know that Allosaurus hunted in packs?

We know from teeth marks on fossilized bones that *Allosaurus* ate *Diplodocus*. Because *Diplodocus* were so huge, a group of *Allosaurus* would have had to work together to bring one down.

Assault on the Salt Flats

The salt flats stretch out to the horizon, glowing in the fierce sunlight as if they are white-hot. The glare all but blinds Big Al. Occasionally, the massive, swaying head of a terrified *Diplodocus* strays across the sun and shades it for a moment, allowing Al to see the thundering bulk of his wounded prey trying so desperately to escape.

But Al doesn't need to see right now. He can smell the blood of the injured *Diplodocus*, sense its fear, and he can hear the baying calls of other *Allosaurus* as they sprint over the salt.

How fast could Allosaurus run?

Experts can tell from fossilized footprints that a dinosaur of Al's size could have run at around 18 miles per hour.

Sudden Strike

The *Diplodocus* cannot keep up the pace.
Cut off from its herd by hungry *Allosaurus,* it finally falls.

The crowd watches greedily, waiting for it to die. But Al's hunger
makes him careless, and he gets too close to the fallen giant.

A single lash of the *Diplodocus*'s tail sends Al tumbling backward.
He roars in pain as he lands badly on his own tail, breaking a
bone. But he's lucky. If the injury was any worse, Al could
find himself in the same position as this dying
Diplodocus—an easy meal for **scavengers.**
He gets back up, painfully.

How can a dinosaur's bones tell us when an injury occurred?

When a bone breaks, it mends itself by growing new bone around the fracture. By looking at such damage with medical scanners, and by examining how well a break has healed, experts can tell when the injury occurred. Al's healed tailbone suggests that he damaged it when he was four or five years old, probably while hunting.

Flesh-Eating Frenzy

As soon as the *Allosaurus* realize the *Diplodocus* is dead, they pounce on it, tearing it apart. Now that their lust for blood has taken over, they no longer work as a team. They snap at each other, squabbling and fighting for the best meat.

Al forgets the pain in his tail as he starts munching on the *Diplodocus*—but suddenly he hears a terrible howling and snarling. The predators all look up, fearfully, to find an enormous female *Allosaurus* approaching. She has smelled the blood of their kill, and now she will use her great size to assert herself and take the best meat.

Al scowls, but he knows his place. He tears off a piece of meat from the *Diplodocus*'s tail and retreats to chew it in safety.

Which were bigger— male or female adult Allosaurus?

Probably the females. Among modern reptiles, female crocodiles and turtles are usually bigger than males because they have to make and carry so many eggs.

A Killer at Six

Another year has gone past in a haze of blood and violence. Big Al is now six years old, and well on the way to becoming an adult.

It is the beginning of the dry season after a long spell of rain, and food is plentiful. Al is washing down his latest meal with water from a stream. Small pterosaurs rush to get out of his way. *Stegosaurus* and *Othnielia* watch nervously as Al approaches, and they are ready to run. But Al is too full of raw meat to chase them right now.

Suddenly, his nostrils twitch. He can smell something, something that never bothered him before, when he was younger. A fully grown female *Allosaurus* is behind him.

Al wants to be friends. For the first time in his life, he shouts out a mating call...

What color were dinosaurs?

The answer is, we don't know! It is probable that, like some modern reptiles, dinosaurs were a similar color to their surroundings. Some dinosaurs may have had flashes of bright color to serve as a warning, or to show that they were mature and ready to mate. And others may have had dull grayish or greenish colors to act as heat reflectors.

Savage Struggle

The female *Allosaurus* is older than Al—bigger, too. Under her bloodred brows, her cold yellow eyes are fixed on him.

Al comes closer, but the female doesn't want to mate. She rushes at him, snarling and hissing. She butts his head, and Al feels the sickening crack of bone on bone. Reeling, he feels a terrible pressure on his arm, twisting him around. Is it her teeth, her claws? Al doesn't know, but suddenly he's on his back, in shock and burning with pain.

The *Allosaurus* towers above him. She lifts one huge foot and stamps down hard on Al's ribs, breaking his bones with a splintering crack. Al snaps out of his daze as the noise and pain tell him he must start running for his life. The female's massive head swoops down, her needle-sharp teeth biting Al's throat, but he rolls away and sprints for the cover of the forest.

The female *Allosaurus* watches him go, bellowing in victory.

How do we know how different wounds were caused?

By looking at the types of breaks in bones. A cross-section of Al's right hand showed it had been broken all along its length. This suggests that it was snapped by a twisting force, which could only have happened in a fight. With broken ribs dating from the same period, it seems likely that Al got them in the same struggle, quite possibly while trying to mate.

Dry Danger

Five months later, Al's wounds have not yet healed. He still cannot use his injured hand. The dry weather has continued, and the heat of the sun is scorching. Rivers that were once wide and welcoming have dwindled to trickles in the baking earth.

A pterosaur perches on the sticky bones of a dead dinosaur, pecking at the few tough scraps of meat still clinging to it—and never hears Big Al creeping up behind. With a crack, the pterosaur's wing snaps in Al's jaws, and the pterosaur struggles to escape.

But Al's teeth close on its skull, crunching through it as if it's an eggshell.

There is not much meat on the pterosaur. Big Al needs more food in order to survive. However much his body hurts, he must go hunting.

Al's nose twitches as he scents other animals nearby. He spies a small herd of *Othnielia*, rooting in the parched earth for scrubby plants. His mouth begins to water. He narrows his eyes, readies himself for the charge…

How do we know Big Al had so many problems hunting?

Al was either unlucky, clumsy, or very aggressive! His fossilized skeleton is the most damaged that experts have ever seen, with 19 bones either broken or injured. It's likely he picked up these injuries while he was at his most active, during times of hunting.

The Fatal Attack

Now. Al rushes for the *Othnielia*. Their nimble bodies are blurs of green as they dart off in terror. He targets one, the youngest and the fattest. His jaws snap. He's gaining…*gaining*.

Then it happens. Al trips and crashes into the dusty ground. He roars in agony—it feels as if lightning has struck his right foot. He struggles to get up, but he sees the *Othnielia* disappearing in the distance. The attack has failed, and it has cost him dearly.

Al shrieks in pain and confusion as he tries to put his weight on his bad foot. His middle toe is broken. Hot and hungry, all he can do is limp slowly away.

A broken toe doesn't sound all that serious. Was it?

A broken toe must have been a disaster for Al. In the modern world, ostriches, which have similar feet to *Allosaurus*, often break their toes from tripping on uneven ground. Then, unable to spread their weight through their feet, they can hardly walk. The fossil evidence shows that Al would have been in exactly the same situation.

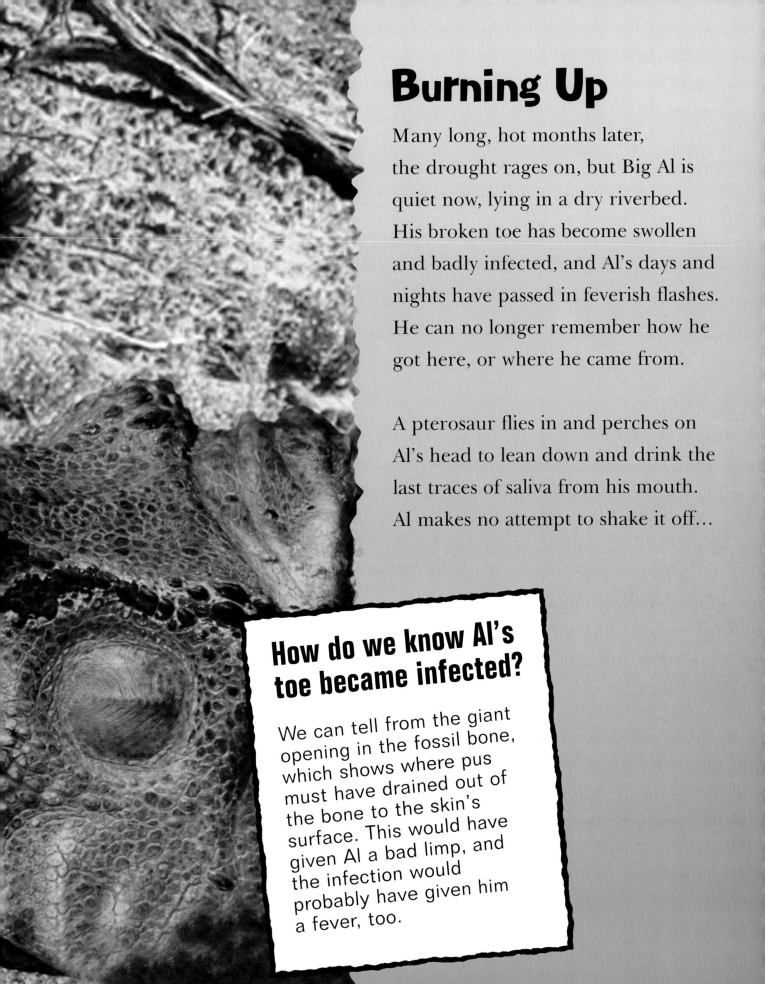

Burning Up

Many long, hot months later, the drought rages on, but Big Al is quiet now, lying in a dry riverbed. His broken toe has become swollen and badly infected, and Al's days and nights have passed in feverish flashes. He can no longer remember how he got here, or where he came from.

A pterosaur flies in and perches on Al's head to lean down and drink the last traces of saliva from his mouth. Al makes no attempt to shake it off…

How do we know Al's toe became infected?

We can tell from the giant opening in the fossil bone, which shows where pus must have drained out of the bone to the skin's surface. This would have given Al a bad limp, and the infection would probably have given him a fever, too.

st Moments

breathing becomes heavier,
er. His vision clouds over.
e sun goes on burning down,
yes finally flicker and close.

dead.

the dinosaur's ravaged body
ers one last act of violence,
n in death. After a few more
s lying out in the blistering
at, Al's stomach spectacularly
plodes, punching a hole right
rough his ribs.

How do we know Al died peacefully?

Because if he had been attacked while he was dying, his bones would show bite marks and would be scattered. Only his ribs were found six feet or so away from his otherwise remarkably complete skeleton.

Why did Al's stomach explode?

Experts think that **bacteria** in Al's stomach were broken down as his digestive juices went on working after his death. Eventually a buildup of gas burst open his stomach.

The Burial

The rains finally return to the prehistoric plain, but they have come too late for Big Al.

His burial is very gentle. Fast-flowing waters that once would have soothed Al lift his body as the river runs again. Then, slowly, his giant frame sinks beneath the surface, drifting to the bottom of the riverbed.

The rains fade and the sun returns to warm the world. Pterosaurs flap slowly over the wild river, circling above the towering heads of *Apatosaurus* bathing in the water. In the distance, the cries of nervous *Diplodocus* break the silence, together with the savage roaring of hungry *Allosaurus*. The world goes on.

The mud of the riverbed will cover Al and keep his remains safe and undisturbed for 145 million years, until they are discovered in Shell, Wyoming, in 1991.

How do we know Al was buried by a river?

Geologists think that the rock that held Al's body had been severely dried out and then saturated with water—a sure sign of a severe drought followed by a flood.

Big Al – His Story Lives On

As millions of years passed, the world's landscape changed. Continents formed out of the huge clump of land that had sat in the middle of the prehistoric ocean and had been home to Al. The vast plains where he lived vanished, and mountains grew up to take their place. Eventually, Al's remains were revealed when the earth that held him was blown aside by the wind and then washed away by water. With 95 percent of his skeleton intact, he was a dream find for dinosaur experts.

A cast of Al's bones is mounted at the Wyoming University Geological Museum. His life was short and savage, but in death he has helped us understand much more about the wild and dangerous world in which he stuggled to survive.

Through the telling of his story, Al lives on.

Fact File

Allosaurus

Pronounced AL-uh-SAW-rus

A powerful, meat-eating dinosaur of the Jurassic period with strong claws and over 70 long teeth to tear apart its victims. *Allosaurus* grew to be almost 40 feet long and stood more than 16 feet tall. It weighed up to three tons.

Allosaurus fossils have been discovered in the United States of America in Wyoming, Utah, and New Mexico, and in Tanzania. Close relatives have also been found in Australia and Portugal.

Apatosaurus

Pronounced a-PAT-uh-SAW-rus

A massive, long-necked herbivore of the Jurassic period. It grew to be up to 115 feet long and weighed around 39 tons.

Archaeopteryx

Pronounced ark-i-OPT-uh-rix

The oldest confirmed bird fossil is of *Archaeopteryx*. It had a skeleton that is very similar to that of a meat-eating dinosaur called *Compsognathus*, but it also had feathers. Experts think that birds descended from dinosaurs sometime during the Jurassic period. *Archaeopteryx* lived 150 million years ago and was the size of a small chicken.

Bacteria

Single-celled small organisms. Some bacteria are parasites—they live inside other living things and feed on them. But most live in water, in the air, in the soil, and even deep within rocks. In fact, everywhere.

Brachiosaurus
Pronounced BRAK-ee-uh-SAW-rus

A massive herbivore of the Jurassic period that could grow as heavy as 78 tons. Its long neck allowed it to feast on vegetation from treetops.

Carnivore
Any animal that feeds on other animals

Cretaceous period

A period of time that spanned from 146 million to 65 million years ago, during which the continents separated to form Laurasia and Gondwana. At the end of this period, dinosaurs became extinct.

Deinonychus
Pronounced dy-NON-i-kus

A fearsome, fast-moving carnivore that lived in the Cretaceous period. It had a movable, sickle-shaped toe claw on each foot that could be used to gouge flesh from its prey.

Dinosaur

A kind of reptile that walked on land in the Mesozoic era, now extinct. The word *dinosaur* means "terrible reptile," and was first used by the British anatomist Sir Richard Owen in 1842 to describe a particular type of prehistoric reptile, whose bones he had discovered. These dinosaurs were different from other reptiles because of their special hipbones. They had legs that were upright like a bird's, instead of being splayed like a crocodile's. As more and more fossil remains were discovered with this small but important difference, it became clear that the dinosaurs had actually ruled as the dominant life form in our world for a period of 160 million years. It is likely that less than 10 percent of all the different dinosaurs that once lived have actually been identified.

Diplodocus
Pronounced di-PLOH-duh-kus

One of the largest of all dinosaurs, a herbivore of the Jurassic period with a lengthy tail and neck. It grew to be up to 148 feet long and weighed up to 34 tons.

Fossils
Bits of prehistoric bones and bodies that have been found in the ground, gradually having turned to stone over millions of years. They are most likely to be found in regions where the sediments and sands spread by rivers of the Mesozoic era lie exposed.

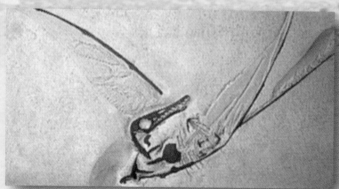

Everything we know about dinosaurs, we know from fossils.

Geologist
Someone who studies the history, structure, and composition of rocks

Hatchling
A young creature, only recently hatched from its egg

Herbivore
Any animal that feeds on plants

Jurassic period

PANGAEA

A period of time spanning from 208 million to 146 million years ago, during which the supercontinent Pangaea began to break up and land that used to be desert became lush and green

Mesozoic era
The so-called era of middle animals, also known as the age of reptiles, is the period of time that covers the **Triassic**, **Jurassic**, and **Cretaceous** periods, the time when the dinosaurs lived.

Ornitholestes
Pronounced ORN-ith-UL-es-TEES

A meat-eating dinosaur with a crest on its nose and spiny quills running down the back of its neck. It grew to be up to 8 feet long and weighed up to 26 pounds.

Othnielia

Pronounced oth-NEE-eh-lee-ah

A relatively large herbivore. Its horny beak cropped low-growing vegetation, and its stiff tail helped it balance when running. It grew to be up to 13 feet long and weighed up to 40 pounds.

Predator

Any meat-eating animal that hunts its prey

Pterosaur

Pronounced TERR-uh-SAW

The name given to any extinct reptile that flew through the air in the Mesozoic era

Reptile

A cold-blooded creature typically covered in scales or plates. Reptiles today include snakes, lizards, crocodiles, and turtles.

Scavenger

An animal that feeds on things that have been discarded, or that are dead. A modern example of a scavenger is a rat.

Stegosaurus

Pronounced STEG-uh-SAW-rus

A heavily armored herbivore of the Jurassic period with a brain smaller than a Ping-Pong ball! It grew to be up to 39 feet long and weighed up to 8 tons.

Triassic period

PANGAEA

A period of time spanning from 250 million to 208 million years ago, during which the first dinosaurs appeared, living on one huge supercontinent, Pangaea

Tyrannosaurus rex

Pronounced tye-RAN-uh-SAW-rus RECKS

One of the most aggressive dinosaurs that ever walked the Earth, with teeth the size of bananas!

Velociraptor

Pronounced vel-OSS-ee-RAP-tor

A medium-size and vicious dinosaur that belongs to the same group of dinosaurs as Deinonychus, and was a very fast and efficient hunter

Credits

Adapted by Stephen Cole
Designed by Matthew Lilly

Discovery Communications, Inc.
John S. Hendricks, Founder, Chairman, and Chief Executive Officer
Judith A. McHale, President and Chief Operating Officer
Clark Bunting II, Executive Vice President and General Manager,
Animal Planet
Judy L. Harris, Senior Vice President, Consumer and Educational
Products

Discovery Publishing
Stephen Newstedt, Vice President
Rita Mullin, Editorial Director
Michael Hentges, Art Director
Mary Kalamaras, Senior Editor
Rick Ludwick, Managing Editor

Discovery Kids ™ is a trademark of Discovery Communications, Inc.

Published in the United States 2001 by Dutton Children's Books,
a division of Penguin Putnam Books for Young Readers
345 Hudson Street, New York, New York 10014
www.penguinputnam.com

Printed in Singapore

First American Edition
2 4 6 8 10 9 7 5 3 1
ISBN 0-525-46773-4

Acknowledgments
BBC Worldwide Limited wishes to
thank the BBC Natural History Unit Picture Library
for the use of the photograph on page 9 (top left)
and Scott W. Rogers, Ph.D., Associate Professor,
University of Utah School of Medicine,
for the use of the photograph on page 18 (top right).

BBC Worldwide Limited also wishes to thank Kate Bartlett,
Paul Chambers, paleontologist, Alex Freeman, animal behavioralist,
and GEAL—Museum of Lourinha, Portugal, for their assistance.

Scientific adviser to BBC Worldwide: Professor Michael J. Benton,
Department of Earth Sciences, University of Bristol